Tennyson
A dreamer and a poet.

Mrs H
A smile and a snack for everyone.

Twigs
Ready to learn and play every day.

CWR, Waverley Abbey House, Waverley Lane, Farnham, Surrey GU9 8EP

National Distributors
UK (and countries not listed below): CWR, PO Box 230, Farnham, Surrey GU9 8XG. Tel: (01252) 784710   Outside UK (44) 1252 784710
AUSTRALIA: CMC Australasia, PO Box 519, Belmont, Victoria 3216. Tel: (03) 5241 3288
CANADA: CMC Distribution Ltd, PO Box 7000, Niagara on the Lake, Ontario L0S 1J0. Tel: (0800) 325 1297
GHANA: Challenge Enterprises of Ghana, PO Box 5723, Accra. Tel: (021) 222437/223249 Fax: (021) 226227
HONG KONG: Cross Communications Ltd, 1/F, 562A Nathan Road, Kowloon. Tel: 2780 1188 Fax: 2770 6229
INDIA: Crystal Communications, 10-3-18/4/1, East Marredpally, Secunderabad – 500 026. Tel/Fax: (040) 7732801
KENYA: Keswick Bookshop, PO Box 10242, Nairobi. Tel: (02) 331692/226047
MALAYSIA: Salvation Book Centre (M) Sdn Bhd, 23 Jalan SS 2/64, 47300 Petaling Jaya, Selangor.
Tel: (03) 78766411/78766797 Fax: (03) 78757066/78756360
NEW ZEALAND: CMC New Zealand Ltd, Private Bag, 17910 Green Lane, Auckland. Tel: (09) 5249393 Fax: (09) 5222137
NIGERIA: FBFM, Helen Baugh House, 96 St Finbarr's College Road, Akoka, Lagos. Tel: (01) 7747429/4700218/825775/827264
PHILIPPINES: OMF Literature Inc, 776 Boni Avenue, Mandaluyong City. Tel: (02) 531 2183 Fax: (02) 531 1960
REPUBLIC OF IRELAND: Scripture Union, 40 Talbot Street, Dublin 1. Tel: (01) 8363764
SINGAPORE: Campus Crusade Asia Ltd, 315 Outram Road, 06-08 Tan Boon Liat Building, Singapore 169074. Tel: (065) 222 3640
SOUTH AFRICA: Struik Christian Books, 80 MacKenzie Street, PO Box 1144, Cape Town 8000. Tel: (021) 462 4360 Fax: (021) 461 3612
SRI LANKA: Christombu Books, 27 Hospital Street, Colombo 1. Tel: (01) 433142/328909
TANZANIA: CLC Christian Book Centre, PO Box 1384, Mkwepu Street, Dar es Salaam. Tel: (051) 2119439
UGANDA: New Day Bookshop, PO Box 2021, Kampala. Tel: (041) 255377
ZIMBABWE: Word of Life Books, Shop 4, Memorial Building, 35 S Machel Avenue, Harare. Tel: (04) 781305 Fax: (04) 774739

For e-mail addresses, visit the CWR web site: www.cwr.org.uk

Tails: Almost Christmas

© 2001 Karyn Henley. All rights reserved. Exclusively administered by Child Sensitive Communication, LLC
Text and characterisations by Karyn Henley
Models created by: Debbie Smith
Photographed by: Roger Walker
Illustrator: Sheila Anderson Hardy of Advocate
Designer: Christine Reissland at CWR
Editor: Lynette Brooks
Printed in Spain by Espace Grafic Navarra
ISBN 1 85345 185 1
Published 2001 by CWR

All rights reserved. No part of this publication may be reproduced, stored in a retrieval system, or transmitted, in any form or by any means, electronic, mechanical, photocopying, recording or otherwise, without the prior permission in writing of CWR.

Almost Christmas

"For God loved the world so much that he gave his only Son"
John 3:16

Karyn Henley

Almost Christmas

Snowflakes drifted past Owlfred's windows. Indoors, Tennyson watched as Owlfred flew up and placed a star on top of the Christmas tree.

"Almost finished!" said Owlfred, fluttering down. He hung three silver bells on the tree. Tennyson placed two candles on the table.

"What are you bringing to the party tomorrow night?" Owlfred asked.

"A ... a ... a surprise!" Tennyson said.

The truth was Tennyson hadn't thought about bringing anything. But he left Owlfred's house thinking a good deal about it.

Down the path came Chester, carrying a wreath. "Merry Christmas Tennyson!" Chester called.

"Merry Christmas!" said Tennyson. "Chester, what are you bringing to Owlfred's party?"

"Games and mistletoe!" said Chester. "What are you bringing?"

"Um … it's a surprise!" said Tennyson.

Just then they heard carollers singing Christmas songs. "Let's go listen!" said Chester.

"You go," said Tennyson. "I have to work on my surprise."

"All right," said Chester. "See you at the party!"

Tennyson walked on, deep in thought. He wondered what the Hedgehogs were bringing.

Gingerbread men lined the table at the Hedgehogs' house. Mimi and Twigs were painting faces on them with icing.

"Jolly days and holly days!" said Tennyson.

"Merry Christmas!" said Mrs H.

"I'm just pouring a cup of hot chocolate for Twigs before he goes to bed. Would you like to join him?"

"Not for bedtime, but yes for hot chocolate!" said Tennyson.

"Can't I stay up?" Twigs asked. "I can wrap presents or put sweets on the gingerbread men to make eyes!"

Mrs H shook her head and laughed. "You have a hundred reasons not to go to bed!" she said. "I can tell it's almost Christmas!"

"What's everyone bringing to Owlfred's party?" asked Tennyson, sipping his drink. "Candy canes!" said Twigs. "Gingerbread men," said Mrs H. "Red Christmas flowers!" said Mimi. "What are you bringing?"

"A surprise!" said Tennyson. It sounded good, but what would the surprise be?

That night, Tennyson thought and thought.

He thought all the next day.

He even thought on his way to the party.

But he still couldn't decide what to bring.

At the party there were Christmas flowers and mistletoe ...

... games, gingerbread men and candy canes.

After a while, Owlfred said, "Gather around. I have brought something very special to our party. I have a story."

"Long ago, a little donkey walked the long road to Bethlehem, carrying a young woman named Mary. Her husband Joseph led the donkey. But there was no room for them in Bethlehem, except in a stable.

Of course, the donkey knew all along that that was the best place to stay. But he never expected what happened next – Mary had a baby. God's Son, Jesus, was born.

The animals in the stable were the first to see Him. God loved the world so much that He sent His Son to be with us."

Mimi sighed, "Mistletoe ... gingerbread ... they're all so much fun. But most of all I do love hearing the story of Baby Jesus. I can tell it's almost Christmas!"

Suddenly Tennyson smiled. Why hadn't he thought of it before? He **had** brought something to the party. "Now for my gift," he said. And he began to sing.

One star upon the Christmas tree,
Two candles shining merrily,
Three silver bells, hear them ring!
I can tell it's almost Christmas!

  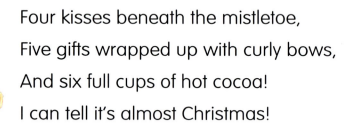

Four kisses beneath the mistletoe,
Five gifts wrapped up with curly bows,
And six full cups of hot cocoa!
I can tell it's almost Christmas!

Bows and tinsel and twinkling lights!
I love all the Christmas sights,
Dancing days and dream-filled nights,
Christmas is almost here.

Seven sweet and swirly candy canes,
Eight wreaths on frosty windowpanes,
Nine carollers sing along the lane!
I can tell it's almost Christmas!

Ten flowers blooming cherry-red,
Eleven men made out of gingerbread,
A hundred reasons not to go to bed,
I can tell it's almost Christmas!

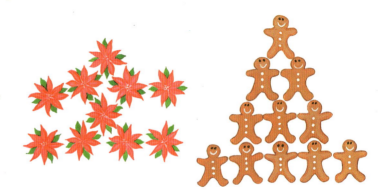

Bows and tinsel and twinkling lights!
I love all the Christmas sights,
Dancing days and dream-filled nights,
Christmas is almost here.

Skies full of angels singing praise.
God's Son is born this very day!
Come! Everyone – see the babe!
He's the greatest gift God gave us!

Yes! Baby Jesus is the One.
He's God's own perfect, holy Son.
He came to show us God's great love.
He's the greatest gift God gave us!

Everyone clapped.

"What a wonderful Christmas surprise!" said Owlfred.

"Yes!" said Tennyson. "It even surprised me!"

If you would like to sing Tennyson's Christmas song, here are the words and the music.

And a very Merry Christmas from your Tails friends!

"For God loved the world so much that he gave his only Son."

John 3:16